Inspired by Grace

VANESSA W. BONNER

AuthorHouse™
1663 Liberty Drive
Bloomington, IN 47403
www.authorhouse.com
Phone: 1 (800) 839-8640

Published by AuthorHouse 03/18/2015

ISBN: 978-1-5049-0183-3 (sc)
ISBN: 978-1-5049-0184-0 (e)

Print information available on the last page.

Any people depicted in stock imagery provided by Thinkstock are models, and such images are being used for illustrative purposes only. Certain stock imagery © Thinkstock.

This book is printed on acid-free paper.

Contents

❦ Acknowledgement ❦

With Special Thanks

To my Lord and Savior Jesus Christ who inspired me to write this book

To my husband Ronald for his love and support. Thank you for believing in the vision God has given us.

To my sons and other family members for all their love, patience and support

To the Pastors who have mentored and encouraged me to use all my the gifts. I thank God for each of you.

To Lonnie and Ruby Perkins for your patience and support in editing and computer software. Thank you.

To Rubbie Borden for your love and support in assisting with editing a third book. Thank you so much.

To my sister midwives. Thank you always for your prayers. May God personally reward each of you.

To my church family and all who have supported this work in any way. Thank you and may the grace of God visit you in a miraculous way.

❦ Introduction ❧

The Word of God says that *we are saved by grace through faith; and that not of ourselves; it is the gift* of *God (Ephesians 2:8).* The gift of God- how wonderfully defined.

There are only two words that can describe this kind of grace: Jesus Christ. We can talk about favor. We can talk about mercy; but unless we begin with the One who died to bring us this grace, we will never know fully of grace.

Over two thousand years ago, Grace came down from heaven wrapped in a blanket. He died on a cross and gave His life for you and me. That's grace.

God's grace manifest gifts of life, peace, joy, and abundance. It is the gift that keeps on giving. You can not receive this grace in your life and remain the same.

I am so thankful that in spite of my imperfections, God still loves me and chooses to show His grace, (His favor) in my life. He continues to inspire me to follow my dreams and to walk in the paths He has chosen for me.

However, God is not a respect of persons. He has favored you to live this life of supernatural abundance. We must choose whether we will receive or reject this free gift of grace. Genuine gifts are never forced.

I pray that this devotional *Inspired by Grace* will be an instrument God will use to deepen your knowledge of Him and release the Power of His Grace in your life.

❦ Dedication ❧

I dedicate this book to the Love of my life; my Lord and Savior Jesus Christ. This is my personal memoir of thanksgiving, praise and acknowledgement for the abundance of grace I have experienced.

Also to our beautiful grandchildren who bring so much joy to our hearts. We are truly blessed to be a part of your lives. We thank God for each of you.

This gift from God
You can't deny
When you see God's love
Within their eyes

God's Vision for You

The former things are come to pass
And new things He doth declare
He promises before they spring forth
He will already be there

He will tell you of the paths-
The things He has for you
He will not leave you in the dark
But will make all things new

God grace us vision to look ahead
To trust You with our lives
As we follow in Your footsteps
And in Your Word abide

The former things are come to pass
They did not come to stay
But they reveal to us what God is doing
In our new and perfect day

Behold, the former things are come to
pass, and new things do I declare: before
they spring forth I tell you of them.

Isaiah 42:9

Endless Love

O' the grace of endless love
I give to you today
As you put your trust in Me
And take heed to what I say

I will do the impossible
I will work miracles through and through
As you keep your focus steadfast on Me
I will fix these things for you

Things entangled: things ensnared
I'll straighten out each one
I won't stop the process
Until this work is done

It is through My mercy
And through My blood

You will know the Grace of endless love

And of his fullness have all we
received, and grace for grace.
St. John 1:16

And out of his fullness(abundance) we have all received {all had a share and we were all supplied with} one grace after another *and* spiritual blessing upon spiritual blessing *and* even favor upon favor and gift {heaped} upon gift.

St. John 1:16/ Amplified Bible

Gifts

Acknowledge every gift
God has given to you
Some gifts are lying dormant
You may not have a clue

These gifts are given
To you through Christ
They will help not only you
But will give others new life

Acknowledge every gift
Don't throw out a thing
What God has placed in you
Will bring great change

We must confess the Word
That God has said
Cast down negative thoughts
Lingering in our head

When we acknowledge God
In every good thing
His kingdom will come
We will never be the same

So don't hide your gift under a bushel
Nor hide it under the bed
God knows what He's placed in you
Don't listen to your head

Your gift might be a simple smile
Perhaps a warm embrace
It might be a listening ear
To encourage someone on their way

It may be a dance or even a song
If it's used for the kingdom
You can never go wrong

Whether it's a card or letter
Or a word in print
God will get all the glory
If men are drawn unto Him

CAUTION:
Never compare your gift to others
Or think its something small
When God places His Spirit in you
It makes you a giant to all!

**That the communication of thy
faith may become effectual by
the acknowledging of every
good thing which is in you
in Christ Jesus**

Philemon 1:6

Wonderful Grace

Grace grace
Wonderful grace
He has given to us
For this marvelous race

Victory and joy
So many mercies in store
God has given us the grace
Of so much more

In this year of Purpose
Visions and Dreams
God won't see us lack
For any good thing

Rest and peace
Grace grace grace
He has given to us
For this marvelous race

Now unto him that is able to do
exceeding abundantly above all that we
ask or think, according to the power
that worketh in us,

Ephesians 3:20

Will You

Will you walk with me
Will you hold my hand
As we move toward our promiseland

Will you pray with me when enemies rise
Will you stand and fight along by my side

When I pull out my sword
Will you do the same
As we destroy principalities
in Jesus name

Or will you run away to the other side
When I'm not looking- will
you run and hide

Will you walk with me
Will you take a stand

As we both press into our Promiseland

Can two walk together,
except they be agreed?

Amos 3:3

The House That Love Built

The house that love built
It's mighty sweet
The entrance is inviting
Its pathways are deep

You won't find it cluttered
You won't find it in a mess
It's always being cleansed
To look its very best

The rooms are aligned with peace
And filled with heaven's praises
God's glory is the light within
With a brightness that's so amazing

Music is playing
The worship is deep
In an atmosphere of thanksgiving
Where blessings you reap!

Ye also as lively stones, are built up
a spiritual house, an holy priesthood,
to offer up spiritual sacrifices,
acceptable to God by Jesus Christ.

1 Peter 2:5

This Holy Place

I will not leave this holy place
Filled with glory -Filled with grace

I will not move nor be ashamed
As I call upon Your wonderful name

Wonderful, Counselor, my Prince of Peace
You cause troubles to vanish
Storms to cease

I will not move from this holy place
Of heavenly worship and warm embrace

I will not allow fear or doubt to replace
The new mercies You have given me
Freely through Your grace

I will not leave this holy place
Of heavenly joy and warm embrace

And he said, Draw not nigh hither:
put off thy shoes from off thy feet, for
the place whereon thou standest
is holy ground.

Exodus 3:1-5

Heavenly Dew

O' the early morning sweetness
Of the heavenly dew
As I arise Lord Jesus
To commune with You

Heaven wraps its arms around me
Arms so tender and strong
O' the joy my heart experiences
In the sweetness of the morn

O God, thou art my God; early will I
seek thee: my soul thirsteth for thee,
my flesh longeth for thee in a dry and
thirsty land, where no water is;

Psalm 63:1

Speak the Word

A man is satisfied by the
words of his mouth
When the enemy comes knocking
Choose to speak life

Our healing and prosperity
Are in the words that we say
We must ask God to help us
So we won't be led astray

In the words that we speak
Our destinies we declare
When we choose to speak life
God's inheritance we will share

A man is made happy
By the words of his mouth
When the enemy comes knocking
Choose to speak life

A man's belly shall be satisfied with
the fruit of his mouth; and with the
increase of his lips shall he be satisfied.

Death and life are in the power
of the tongue: and they that love
it shall eat the fruit thereof.

Proverbs 18:20-21

Lord, I really need to hear You speak
Can you tell me honestly-
What's going on with me
I don't care if it's in a poem: I
don't care if it's in a song
I just want to know - can you
tell me what is wrong

Many disappointments have
come in this season
To cast a shadow of doubt or fear
To convince you otherwise
But I have always been near

In every struggle I've stood close
To make certain you did not fall
There was never a time
That I was not there
When to Me your voice did call

There's nothing that you'll go through
That My grace will not prepare
I tell you again- I give you my promise
I will never leave you - I
will always be there

I was the One who held your hand
And wiped the tears from your eyes
When you were overwhelmed
And to Me your voice- you cried

You are my special delight
The apple of my eye
You are the one to whom I sent
My Son to bleed and die

Don't think for a moment
That I don't know the value of your soul
Don't be so quick to judge and condemn
The one I gave my all

Rest in me- trust in me
Wait upon Me and you will see
Your heart will be lifted
Your mind made free

I am the One- the only One
Who can do what you need done
I am the One - the only One
Who knows how it needs to be done

So relax and rest
My presence you will enjoy
I will give you victory after victory
And so much more

For I know the thoughts that I think
toward you, saith the Lord, thoughts of
peace, and not of evil, to give you an
expected end.

Jeremiah 29:11

If You Believe

If you can believe
His glory you will see
If you can just trust Him
New heights you will be

Miracles, signs, and wonders
As His presence draws near
Faith to believe the impossible
Will erase every tear

If you can believe
New mercies you will know
God's goodness will follow you
In every place you go

Jesus said unto her, Said I not unto
thee, that, if thou wouldest believe,
thou shouldest see the glory of God?

St. John 11:40

The Gifts

Lord
I thank You for the gifts
That You have entrusted me
Gifts that initially I could not see

Their value- their purpose
Were all in Your plan
To bring back to Yourself
The heart of man

All the gifts You have given
All the love You have shown
Was to make it perfectly
And infinitely known

That God who loved the world
Who gave His only Son
Will bend His ear from heaven
To hear the cry of merely one

You are the one He is calling
His voice is in Your ear
You are the one He is seeking
To bring Your heart much nearer

In the last days God says
Perilous times shall come
To keep us from His presence
To keep us on the run

To run from this
To run to that
Not allowing time to pray
Even when we lay down at night
In a moment- it seems it's day

We must heed the Master's warning
To prepare for His return
He said it'd be *as a thief in the night*
That is how He would come

Watch therefore: for ye know not
what hour your Lord doth come.

Matthew 24:42

Lord Don't Let Me Be Found Sleeping
Sleeping At The Door

Let me be a faithful watchman
As You have taught me to
Let me be found doing
The things You've asked me to do

Don't let me be dull of hearing
Or fail to walk in love
Don't let me be lazy about praying
And lose my ultimate reward

Lord let me be a worshipper
A worshipper indeed
Let me live a life
That is born down on my knees

Lord let me be a doer
Of the words that I hear
Let me live a righteous life
One of godly fear

But Lord don't let me be found begging
And crying out for more
While you find me continually sleeping
Sleeping at the door

Ye are all the children of light, and the children of the day: we are not children of the night, nor of darkness.

Therefore let us not sleep, as do others; but let us watch and be sober.

1Thessalonians 5:5-6

Thanksgiving

Praise is a choice
Thanksgiving is a gift
To know that you've been chosen
For such a time as this

Think it not a small thing
This gift God has given you
Think it not significant
Its value tried and true

To be truly thankful
Is the gift God gives to us
To see if we are truly grateful
To God this is a must

To him who has -there shall be given
A heart of genuine joy
Every time you turn around
God will give you more

Praise is a choice
Thanksgiving is a gift
To know that you're chosen and called
For such a time as this

Thanks be unto God for his
unspeakable gift.
11 Corinthians 9:15

For if thou altogether holdest thy peace at this time, *then* shall there enlargement and deliverance arise to the Jews from another place; but thou and thou father's house shall be destroyed: and who knoweth whether thou art come to the kingdom for such a time as this?

Esther 4:14

Love Won't Let Me Wait

Love won't let me wait
I see my lover at the gate

He's calling out to me to come
Now I see Him - I must run

My lover is so grand
Bypassing the love of any man

If you saw what I saw
Knew what I know

Off with your heels
You'd go go go

I see my lover at the gate
He's calling my name

I can't be late

The voice of my beloved! behold,
he cometh leaping upon the
mountains, skipping upon the hills.
My beloved spake, and said unto me, Rise
up, my love, my fair one, and come away.

Song of Solomon 2:8, 10

Taste and See

David tasted of His goodness
John did too
Mary poured out her alabaster box
Before she was through

Now this I must confess
I truly understand
I can't help myself either
I just love the man

Not only do I love Him
I'm in love with Him too
It's a love that's pure
It's a love that's true

I don't always love Him
The way that I should
Still I've tasted of His kindness
I've tasted of His good

If you have not told Him
That you love Him today
Tell Him that you love him
Before you turn the page....

(He's waiting)

**O taste and see that the Lord is good:
blessed is the man that trusteth in him.**

Psalm 34:8

**How sweet are thy words unto my taste!
yea, *sweeter* than honey to my mouth.**

Psalm119:103

**If so be ye have tasted that
the Lord is gracious.**

1 Peter 2:3

Trusting in You

Lord I'm trusting in You
To take me there
To that place of peace
A place without care

No care of the future
No care of the past
No care about problems
Or how long they will last

My eyes are focused
Steadfast on You
In every situation
You will bring me through

You are my Alpha and Omega
My beginning and end
You are taking me places
I have never been

I'm trusting in a God
Who can never be late
He is not only the author-
But the finisher of my faith

Being confident of this very thing, that
he which hath begun a good work in
you will perform it until the day of
Jesus Christ
Philippians 1:6

Rivers

Let your river flow through me
Let it flow pure: let it flow free
Rivers of power and glory too
Rivers that come only through You

Remove anything from my life
That would hinder the flow
Lord I want that river to go go go

Let it go out to the hurting
With a passion to proclaim
The power and the victory
That is in your name

Visit me again with Your grace
Cause my heart to be renewed
That I might finish this race

Fill me with the desire
I long for most
To have your rivers flow through me
In the power of the Holy Ghost

In the last day, that great day of the feast,
Jesus stood and cried, saying, If any man
thirst, let him come unto me and drink.

He that believeth on me, as the scripture hath said, out of his belly shall flow rivers of living water.

St. John 7:37-38

One Simple Act

One simple act of obedience
Without questioning why
Can change a person's existence
Can change their whole life

The woman with the alabaster box
She poured on Jesus feet
One simple act of obedience
Can bring miracles to you and me

Just one simple drink of water
Water from Jacob's well
Can give a life time of testimonies
And miracles to tell

Just one simple act of obedience
To the prophet in your life
Can cause your cupboards to overflow
Your wells never to run dry

One simple act of obedience
Without questioning why
Can cause what's dead to be resurrected
And given brand new life

And he that was dead came forth, bound hand and foot with graveclothes: and his face was bound about with a napkin. Jesus saith unto them, Loose him, and let him go. / St. John 11:44

The Letter

God's love letter
He has written to me
That His compassion I'd know
His love I would see

You are mine
I purchased you with my blood
You are mine
Compared to no other love

Open your heart wide
That you may know
I am with you always
Wherever you go

As I was with Moses
I am with you too
I am a faithful God
I will never forsake you

My letter has passed
The test of time
I always always
Take care of what's mine

The Lord hath appeared of old unto me, saying, Yea, I have loved thee with an everlasting love: therefore with lovingkindness have I drawn thee.
Jeremiah 31:3

Thanks A Zillion

I just want to say thank you
Doesn't matter that I said it before
Seems that every time I thank you
You bless me more and more

My heart fills with gladness
That comes from deep within
No matter how often I thank you
I want to thank you again

Thank you for your love and mercy
Thank you for your truth
Thank you for your sacrifice
And all the things you do

Thank you for your patience
And the love you have for me
Thank you for seeing beyond
What my natural eyes can see

Thank you for this gift of salvation
That You have given me
I bow my heart- I bow my knee
God thanks a zillion for loving me
Thank you

For all things are for your sakes,
that the abundant grace might
through the thanksgiving of many
redound to the glory of God.
11 Corinthians 4:15

Real Love

Today I choose to love You
No matter how I feel
Today I choose to worship
To thank You that I'm healed

Today I choose to praise You
To live my life without fear
I know that You are with me
I know Your love is real

Today I choose to bless You
To bring glory to Your name
I know that You are worthy
I know You never change

Today I choose to thank You
And trust You with my life
I know that You are with me
I know You're on my side

Today I choose to love You
In spite of what I feel
I can't live my life without You
I know Your love is real

I will bless the Lord at all times: his praise shall continually be in my mouth.

Psalm 34:1

Simply because.....

We don't need fancy words
They don't always have to rhyme
We don't need a reason to worship
We can worship anytime

We can worship You

Simply because...
You are wonderful
You are worthy
And because we love You

We worship You
Simply because
You are marvelous

We don't need fancy words
It doesn't matter if they rhyme
We can worship because
we love You

**We can worship anytime
Simply because
You are worthy**

**I will love thee, O Lord, my strength.
Psalm18:1**

Worship and Praise

Worship and praise
Go hand in hand
They give us power
To be strong and power to stand

They steer our focus
Just where it should
On a God who is magnificent-
A God who is Good

He is sweeter than honey
He is better than money
He is a God to be cheered
Yet a God to be feared

Worship and praise
Go hand in hand
They give us the power
To be strong and power to stand

I will worship toward thy holy temple, and
praise thy name for thy lovingkindness
and for thy truth: for thou hast magnified
thy word above all thy name.

Psalm 138:2

Never Enough

If I could work enough
To earn His love
I would not need Jesus
I wouldn't need his blood

This may seem strange
I can tell you why
It can never happen
No matter how we try

God wants us to accept
This gift by faith
It's not by our works
It's all by his grace

Accept that the price
Has already been paid
Believe that His blood
Has already been shed

Down on Calvary's cross
Jesus died for you
His hands were nailed
And his feet were too

We can never work enough
To earn His love
It was paid in full
It was done through his blood

For by grace are ye saved
through faith; and that not of
yourselves: it is the gift of God.

Not of works, lest any man should boast.

Ephesians 2: 8-9

He Still Cares

We often think He's forgotten
When He seems so far away
But His love for us is constant
His loyalty He will not betray

The God who once cared- still cares

When your life seems clouded
With storms and rain
God is still working on your behalf
His love remains the same

What looks like broken promises
And even misplaced dreams
Can in reality
Be the making of a rainbow
In the midst of all the pain

Because He still cares

And we know that all things work
together for good to them that love
God, to them who are the called
according to his purpose.
Romans 8:28

And therefore will the Lord wait, that he may be gracious unto you, and therefore will he be exalted, that he may have mercy upon you: for the Lord is a God of judgment: blessed are all they that wait for Him.
Isaiah 30:18

Take a Chance

Now is the time to worship
You don't need to wait
We won't learn to worship
When we enter heaven's gate

Today is the day of salvation
The day of worship and praise
Today our God is worthy
He is worthy all our days

Worthy of our hands being lifted
He's worthy of a dance
Although someone might see you
Be willing to take the chance

Chance that someone hear
The halleluah of your praise
Chance that someone might witness
Your miracle on its way

Obedience brings the miracles
The miracles we need in life
As we take a chance to reach out to him
Through worship and sacrifice

I will call upon the Lord, *who is worthy* to be praised:
so shall I be saved from mine enemies.
Psalm18:3

Abraham's Secret

Abraham left a message
A message to you and me
If we would worship God
His miracles we would see

Abraham knew how to worship
To believe what God had said
To moved beyond his circumstance
To trust his God instead

Those things that were not
He called them into being
Because he believed in hope
His Isaac he was seeing

A God who is faithful
Should be worshipped indeed
Because Abraham paved the way
Through worship
Now we are Abraham's seed

God will give us Isaac's
During the duration of our lives
If we will learn *Abraham's secret*
The secret of sacrifice

And Abraham said to his servants, Settle down and stay here with the donkey, and I and the young man will go yonder and worship, and come again to you.
Genesis 22:5/ Amplified Bible

The Reality of Faith

Now faith is
Not someday faith will be
Faith is the now
Now is the reality

If we want to have faith
We can't put it in the future
Faith is simply the now
Here is the resolution

Faith is not for withholding
Nor for placing on layaway
The reality of faith is now
The reality of faith is today

Now faith is the assurance (the
confirmation, the title deed) of the things
{we} hope for, being the proof of things
{we} do not see *and* the conviction of
their reality {faith perceiving as real fact
what is not revealed to the senses}.

Hebrews 11:1 / Amplified Bible

He Saw It

You may not think it much
But He does
It was just a smile
A mere act of kindness
He saw it

Anyone could have done it
But you did

Anyone could have encouraged
But you did

Anyone could have taken the time
But you did

You may not think it much
But He does

It was just a mere act of kindness
But He saw it

......He saw it

And the King shall answer and say unto them, Verily I say unto you, Inasmuch as ye have done *it* unto one of the least of these my brethren, ye have done it unto me.

Matthew 25:34-40

Action

Love in Action
Is what we need
Love in practice
Helps us succeed

Who wants a love
That can never share
The things I go through
Or the burdens I bare

Who wants a love
That can forever dare
But when it comes to feeling
It does not care

Love in action
Is what we need
If we want real life
If we want to succeed

My little children, let us not love in word,
neither in tongue; but in deed and in truth.

1John 3:18

New Beginnings

It's a new day
It's a new day indeed
To love on Jesus
To plant that seed

To plant the seed of love
Instead of debate
It's a day to start over
To receive a clean slate

Everything we've gone through
Every tear we've ever shed
Jesus has conquered for us
When He rose up from the dead

No longer need we live our lives
In the pain of yesterday
We can have a new beginning
We can have a clean slate

We can plant the seed of love
And live in our new day
For He has declared our victory
He has given to us new grace!

Ye are of God, little children,
and have overcome them:
because greater is he that is in
you, than he that is in the world.

1 John 4:4

Making of a Vessel

You're making me a vessel
A vessel tried and true
A vessel You are preparing
To be used by You

Sometimes I jump and shout
Sometimes it don't feel good
At times I may not respond
The way I really should

Sometimes I may wiggle
Sometimes I may pout
I wish that this trial
You would let me out

I didn't know the scraping
Would hurt this bad
But I look in your eyes
I can't possibly be mad

Because You're making me a vessel
A vessel tried and true
A vessel You're preparing
To be used by You

**And the vessel that he made of clay was marred in the hand of the potter: so he made it again another vessel, as seemed good to the potter to make it.
Jeremiah 18:4**

Center Stage

My heart belongs to You Lord
I worship You today
Above all that is around me
You get center stage

My heart belongs to You Lord
Above the trials that I see
Deep calls unto deep
Your Spirit dwelling inside of me

Calling out I'm here beside you
I have come in you to dwell
I have secrets to entrust you
Mysteries I want to tell

My heart belongs to You Lord
No one knows me like You
Others see upon the surface
But You see through and through

My heart belongs to You, O Lord
As I worship You today
Above all that surround me
You get center stage

Jesus answered and said unto him, If a man love me, he will keep my words: and my Father will love him, and we will come unto him, and make our abode with him.
St. John 14:23

Stay Focused

When things seem
As though they're unclear
Don't become discouraged
Your answer is near

Stay focused

Sometimes it's only a test
But you don't know why
Stay focused

When your heart is glad
When your heart seems sad
Stay focused

Things you don't understand today
Tomorrow may be clear
Keep your focus steadfast on Him
His coming is very near

For yet a little while, and he that shall
come will come, and will not tarry.

Hebrews 10:37

Peace

We must follow after peace
We must treasure it in our heart
We must never minimize its value
Or think its something its not

Peace is not money
It's not fortune or fame
But righteousness, peace, and joy
When we call on His name

Nothing compares to the peace
We have in Christ
No relationship, no vision
Nor any sacrifice

We could have all the money
Our little hearts could receive
Yet none of it would matter
If we had no peace

Peace I leave with you, my peace I
give unto you: not as the world giveth,
give I unto you. Let not your heart be
troubled, neither let it be afraid.

St. John 14:27

Opportunities

Often things happen in our lives
That we don't understand
That tempt us to doubt God's promises
To take matters in our own hands

That's the time to worship
To lift our hands in praise
We'll see God bring deliverance
And bring our hearts new faith

Just like Paul and Silas
God's perfect will may be
To allow an opportunity
So this miracle we will see

And what may seem in life
To be an earthquake's shaking
May actually be God's handy work
Of a miracle in the making

And at midnight Paul and Silas
prayed, and sang praises
unto God: and the prisoners heard them.

And suddenly there was a great earthquake, so that the foundations of the prison were shaken: and immediately all the doors of the prison were opened, and everyone's bands were loosed.
Acts 16:25-26

No Lack

Put your hand to the plow
Don't look back
Ahead is the Promiseland
A place without lack

Spiritual abundance
Financial too
A sweet inheritance that God
Has left for you

Don't allow the giants
To cause you to fear
What God has promised
Is very near

Keep moving forward
Don't look back
God's bringing you to a place
Where there is no lack

Let us hold fast the profession of
our faith without wavering; (for
he is faithful that promised;)

Hebrews 10:23

The Sacrifice of Worship

We serve a worthy God
Who is worthy of our praise
We serve a worthy God
Who is worthy everyday

It doesn't matter when we rise
No matter how we feel
God is worthy of our worship
In spite of how it appears

God made us for worship
He gave His all for us
No matter how long we worship
We can never worship enough

Sometimes it may be a sacrifice
Sometimes it truly is
That's the time we see God move
When we give Him worship that's real

By him therefore let us offer the sacrifice
of praise to God continually, that is, the
fruit of our lips giving thanks to his name.

Hebrews 13:15

Grace and Peace

God's Word is the place
Where grace abides
Where grace and peace
Walk side by side

Through knowledge of the Word
Grace will multiply
As we put our faith in Him
And not our natural eyes

If we meditate in His Word
All our doubts will cease
God will fill us with grace
He will fill us with His peace

We'll grow in God like never before
With Jesus on our side
We'll see our lives changed forever
Through grace and peace multiplied

Grace and peace be multiplied
unto you through the knowledge
of God, and of Jesus our Lord,

11Peter 1:2/ King James Version

Don't Fall Short

Don't fall short this year
Of the grace God has for you
He can do far and beyond
All that you can do

God's grace is extended
It is free to all
It will keep you afloat
It will not let you fall

While you may be frustrated
Tempted to throw up your hands
He's still reaching out to you
He still has a Master plan

Don't try to reason
Don't try to guess
God's plan for you
Is always the best

He has conquered all
Of hell death and the grave
That He might freely come to you
To give you this grace

That in the ages to come he might shew the exceeding riches of his grace in *his* kindness toward us through Christ Jesus.

Ephesians 2:7

Anointed to Win

We are anointed to win
Each and every test
God has promised to help us
Always to do our best

We are created in his image
Redeemed by his blood
We are anointed to prosper
We are anointed to love

All that we need
We have within
God has anointed us with grace
We are anointed to win

Nay, in all these things we are more than
conquerors through him that loved us.

Romans 8:37

Breathe

Breathe in His great love
Breathe in His great mercy
Breathe in His tremendous power
His grace

He is going to cause you to
Rest in His strength
Rest in His Freedom
As He liberates you day to day

That you might breathe in His love
And breathe out the manifesations
Of His mighty power
To a lost and hurting world

Then said Jesus to the again, Peace
be unto you: as *my* Father hath
sent me, even *so* send I you.

And when he had said this, he
breathed on them, and saith unto
them, Receive ye the Holy Ghost:

St. John 20:21-22

The Gift to Know

Grace is the gift to know
God's mercy doth abide
With every sinner and saint alike
No matter how we strive

His gift says "Come to all who labor
And I will give you rest"
He won't give us leftovers
He will always give us His best

The gift to know we're never alone
No matter what we face
The gift to know He'll always be there
To give to us more grace

For God, who commanded the light
to shine out of darkness, hath shined
in our hearts, to give the light of
the knowledge of the glory of God
in the face of Jesus Christ.

11 Corinthians 4:6

Come unto me, all *ye* that labour and are heavy laden, and I will give you rest.

Mathew 11:28

Declare and Decree
(Dialogue)

I know what You've promised me
I know as well
Now is the time to declare and decree

But I don't see it you might say
Yes I know
But declare and decree it anyway

When you hear that joyful sound
Plant your seed into the ground

It's by faith you will plant
By faith you will see
As you obey My Word
To declare and decree

It's so simple- but yet profound
If you want to get a harvest
You have to plant your seed in the ground

Thou shalt also decree a thing, and
it shall be established unto thee: and
the light shall shine upon thy ways.

Job 22:28

You Are God Anyway

When you come with correction
While we run this race
We can still rejoice

You are God anyway

What parent does not discipline his child
Or pull him aside to be still for a while

While He pours in his heart
He pours in his ear
The things that only His child
Needs to hear

Unless we come to God as children
Into the kingdom we won't go
It'd do us well to stop our striving
Learn to listen and take it slow

When God comes with correction
As we run this race
We can still rejoice
Because He is God anyway!

Behold, happy is the man whom God correcteth: therefore despise not thou the chastening of the Almighty: For he maketh sore, and bindeth up: he woundeth, and his hands make whole.
Job 5:17-18

Pennies

We habitually count our change
Before we leave the store
To see if there was a mistake
To see if it should be more

But we rush through our worship
We rush out the door
Never checking with the Lord
Did He need to say more

Never checking to see
When the prayer is through
If perhaps there is something
God wanted us to do

So we rush through our worship
We rush out the door
We leave with mere pennies
But God wanted to give us more

For I say unto you, That unto every
one which hath shall be given; and
from him that hath not, even that he
hath shall be taken away from him.

Luke 19:26

79

66 Books

I can't live my life without You
I'd make a mess I'm sure
If I tried to make my own decisions
As though I was secure

As Adam and Eve in the garden
Ignored the words You said
I'd rather avoid the shipwreck
And listen to You instead

Your wisdom You will share
Your understanding too
If I would take the time
To commune with You

In Your Word You have written
Everything I'll ever need
You've placed in sixty-six books
You did it all for me

You gave so many examples
So I could pass the test
When life would come before me
To tempt me with unrest

You placed your Holy Spirit inside me
To guide me along the way
To lead me in the paths of righteousness
To the new and living way

It's all been laid out before us
If we'll only take a look
Our destiny is awaiting us
Written by God in sixty six books

This book of the law shall
not depart out of thy
mouth; but thou shalt meditate day
and night, that thou mayest observe
to do according to all that is
written therein for then will
thou make thy way
prosperous, and then thou
wilt have good success.
Joshua 1:8

Celebration

Today is a day of rejoicing
A day of celebration and praise
To the One who gave His life for me
Who will love me all my days

Today is a day of victory
Jesus our battles have won
Let's follow in His footsteps
Do the things that He has done

Let's love our neighbors
Save the lost
Lay down our lives
At any cost

Open blind eyes so they can see
Change our talk to victory
Unstop deaf ears-raise the dead
Do the greater works like He said

Verily, verily, I say unto you, He that
believeth on me, the works that I do shall
he do also; and greater *works* than these
shall he do; because I go unto my Father.

St. John 14:12

Be a Lover

If you want your heart to feel lighter
Be a lover- not a fighter
If you feel strife coming your way
Run to the altar and pray pray pray

Strife is a major deceiver
It doesn't seem as bad as it looks
But we must remember Judas
And how little it took

For him to walk one day with Jesus
And the serpent the next
That is why his soul
Will eternally be vexed

God says in the last days
The love of many would wax cold
We must be on guard
For this Word we were told

We must avoid strife
At all cost in this hour
If we want to walk with Jesus
If we want to flow in his power

And above all these things *put on* charity,
which is the bond of perfectness.

Colossians 3:14

A New Thing

God's grace is upon me
I'm so thankful today
He has come to reveal to me
His new and perfect way

He's promised He'd do a new thing
I will not question how
I know He's always been faithful
I know He can not lie

Things that hadn't been revealed
My heart is open to see
He's showing me how to trust in Him
And not so much in me

I'm not taking Him for granted
Or rushing out the door
I'm just sitting in His presence
Waiting for Him to show me more

I know that He loves me
I see it in His face
That is why I'm so thankful
I'm so thankful for His grace

For I will set mine eyes on
them for good, and I will
bring them again to this land: and I will
build them, and not pull them down; and
I will plant them, and not pluck them up.

And I will give them a heart to know me,
that I *am* the Lord: and they shall be my
people, and I will be their God: for they
shall return unto me with all their heart.

Jeremiah 24:6-7

Enough is Enough

God made marriage to be sweet
How do we keep messing it up
Blaming Adam- blaming Eve
Hey when is enough enough

God says if we continue in His Word
His Word would make us free
That means I can be responsible
For the Word He's placed in me

You can be responsible
For the Word He's placed in you
We can be about the Father's business
And do what He has told us to do

So it's time to stop blaming
Time to stop shaming
And admit that enough is enough
God made marriage to be sweet as honey

We just have to stop messing it up!

And the rib which the Lord God had taken from man, made he a woman, and brought her unto the man.

And Adam said, This is now bone of my bones, and flesh of my flesh: she shall be called Woman, because she was taken out of Man.

Genesis 2:22-23

God's Grace Is For All

God grace is for you
God's grace is for me
His grace is for our friends
And all our family

To bring us closer and closer
To his perfect will
As we learn to grow together
While our hearts we yield

Like a beautiful flower garden
With multiple colors
We're not all the same
Yet we respect one another

You don't always tell me
What I want to hear
But I trust our friendship
I know it's sincere

In family and godly friendship
Much favor lies
As we honor God's principles
And in His word abide

Greater love hath no *man* than this, that
a man lay down his life for his friends.
St. John 15:13

Friends

Friends like you are very few
Like Jonathan to David
God made you

Like the Apostle John
Who leaned his head
On our Savior's breast

Friends like you
Cause my heart to rest

I don't have to say a word
You know what's on my mind
You have the Father's heart for me
A heart that's tender and kind

Friends like you are very few
Like Jonathan to David
God made you

And when Mephibosheth, the son of
Jonathan, the son of Saul, was come
unto David, he fell on his face, and did
reverence. And David said, Mephibosheth.
And he answered, Behold thy servant!

And David said unto him, Fear not:
for I will surely shew thee kindness
for Jonathan thy father's sake, and
will restore thee all the land of
Saul thy father; and thou shalt eat
bread at my table continually.
11 Samuel 9:6-7

The Blessing of Friendship

What blessings our friends
They do impart
When the Spirit of God
Is in their heart

They bless you with kindness
They bless you with peace
When you leave their presence
Their memories never cease

These blessings continue
They go on and on
The stories will linger
Even after we're gone

God created friendship
To be a part of His plan
When He desired a Family
When He first made man

Ye are my friends, if ye do
whatsoever I command you.

St. John 15:14

The Crucified Life

If we want to partake
Of the sufferings of Christ
We will live more meaningful
Our lives we will crucify

God made us for His purpose
He paid the ultimate cost
That we'd walk in His footsteps
We would daily win the lost

As Jesus sought to save
We would do the same
We'd produce the fruits
Of righteousness
By trusting in His name

For Christ also hath once suffered for
sins, the just for the unjust, that he might
bring us to God, being put to death in
the flesh, but quickened by the Spirit:

1 Peter 3:18

Woman You Better Run

Woman woman
You better run
We can't let the Savior appear
Find our work undone

He says you're very precious
In His sight
And He has chosen you
To be included in this fight

So if you've ever doubted
Doubt no more
Jesus has stepped in
And closed the door

He's closed the door to guilt
He's closed the door to shame
He's covered you with His blood
Given you the power of His name

Woman, woman
You better run run run
Finish what He started
He is surely soon to come

There is neither Jew nor Greek,
there is neither bond nor free,
there is neither male nor female:
for ye are one in Christ Jesus.
Galatians 3:28

Grace for the Battle

God gives grace for each battle
Our battles to win
Grace for our struggles
Without and within

He has made us overcomers
We can pass every test
He has given us His Word
We can receive His rest

We can rest in His love
We can rest in His provision
No matter our circumstance
No matter our decisions

God gives grace for each battle
His Word makes us secure
Whatever temptation comes
He gives us grace to endure

Let us therefore come boldly
unto the throne of grace, that
we may obtain mercy, and find
grace to help in time of need.

Hebrews 4:16

Fire

Lord I want that fire
That you promised me
That will burn out sin
Cause my eyes to see

I want the kind of fire
That causes my heart to pound
When I sense Your presence
Everytime that You're around

I want the kind of fire
That will bring Holy Ghost conviction
I want that fire
That will love you without restriction

I want that fire
That will cause me to cry over sin
And pray without ceasing
For the souls of men

Lord I want that fire
That You promised me
That will heal the sick
That will cause blind eyes to see

I indeed baptize you with water unto repentance: but he that cometh after me is mightier than I, whose shoes I am not worthy to bear: he shall baptize you with the Holy Ghost, and with fire: Matthew 3:11

Patience

This is a lesson of wisdom
That will never grow old
It is in our patience
Possess we our souls

We don't have to live in a strain
Except the lord builds the house
God says our labour is in vain

The wisdom of God is so great
As He tells us to hide away
In the secret place

Where the desires of this world
Grow more and more dim
As we look in His eyes
Keep our focus on Him

God moves in His timing
His ways so above
The ways that we think
The ways that we love

God's protection is hidden
In Words wisdom we are told
And it is in our patience
That we possess our souls

In your patience possess ye your souls.
Luke 21:19

The Great Unveiling

Time out for thinking
Something has to change
Now is the great unveiling

I have to change.....

Doing the same things
The same negative way
Will bring the same negative results
I have to change

So it's time out for thinking
If I do it the same
I will see the change

Time out for hoping
Something has to change
Now is the time of the Great Unveiling
I have to change

Or else....be the same
do the same
stay the same

This is the Great Unveiling!

To everything there is a season, and a time to every purpose under the heaven:

Ecclesiastes 3:1

Pour the Honey

Lord sometimes I must confess
When I go through so much mess
Less my feet begin to slip
Please put some honey on my lips

I know it may not sound spiritual
That I should even ask
I could always look sanctimonious
Or wear perhaps a mask

But Lord some things I go through
Really put me through the test
I need honey on my lips
When I go through so much mess

Draw me closer into your presence
Remind me once again
How Jesus endured like temptations
He got the victory- He did not sin

I know it's not always others
Sometimes I know it's me
Regardless I still need your help
Lord I need your mercy

Remind me Your Word has power
That my feet need never slip
You are grace upon my mouth
You are the honey on my lips

Never Giving Up

Never giving up
On the vision You've shown to me
Never giving up
In spite of what I see

The vision outweighs the natural eye
It demands faith to move
Without questioning why

God does the exceeding
He does the above
That we might experience
His unfailing love

He wants us to acknowledge Him
In all that He says
To trust and believe
That He knows the right way

What is right to Him
May not seem right to us
But we'll see the vision fulfilled
If we never give up!

And the Lord answered me, and said,
Write the vision, and make it plain upon
tables, that he may run that readeth it.

For the vision is yet for an appointed time,
but at the end it shall speak, and not
lie: though it tarry, wait for it; because
it will surely come, it will not tarry.

Habakkuk: 2: 2-3

The Mirror

I went to the mirror
I asked what do I see
Is it fear and doubt
Staring back at me

I went back to the Word
To renew my mind
I needed to go
To spend more time

God's Word is the mirror
He has for you and me
We must meditate upon it
Then we can declare and decree

I went back to the mirror
And what did I see
Nothing but victory
Staring back at me

But we all, with open face beholding
as in a glass the glory of the Lord, are
changed into the same image from glory
to glory, even as by the Spirit of the Lord.

11 Corinthians 3: 18

This One Thing

This one thing we need do
It can't be that hard
When we put our trust
Our hope in God

No matter the hurt
No matter the trauma
God can make all things new
He can erase the drama

However we must believe
We must be willing to let go
Then His miracles of life
To us He will show

He is the mender
Of broken hearts you see
He knows how to pour the oil
He is the Remedy

This one thing
We must make up our minds
We can't move forward
While looking behind

Healing is healing
Whatever it be
Forty stripes on His back
Was healing for me

Brethren, I count not myself to have apprehended: but *this* one thing I do, forgetting those things which are behind, and reaching forth unto those things which are before, I press toward the mark for the prize of the high calling of God in Christ Jesus.

Philippians 3:13-14

Is there no balm in Gilead; is there no physician there? why then is there not the health of the daughter of my people recovered?

Jeremiah 8:22

Take Note

Have you met This Blessed Savior
Have you met This Blessed hope
Have you peeked inside the scriptures
Have you ever taken note

Have you met This Wonderful Savior
Full of grace and peace
Did you know He is the One
Who causes hearts to mend
Who causes troubles to cease

Have you met This Wonderful Savior
This Omnipotent- Blessed Hope
He is the One who really loves us
Have you ever taken note

Come see a man, which told me all things
which ever I did: is not this the Christ?

St. John 4:29

Prodigals

There are some prodigals
Who leave home
To do a different dance
They may or may not return
But still they take the chance

Prodigals come home
The Father is calling your name
It doesn't matter what you've done
He loves you just the same

Prodigal come home
He knows what you need
He knows how to love you
He knows how to make you succeed

I can feel his heart
See the tears on His face
As He's beckoning you to come
While you still have the grace

And he arose, and came to his father. But
when he was yet a great away off, his
father saw him, and had compassion, and
ran, and fell on his neck, and kissed him.

St. Luke 15:20

❧ My Testimony of Grace ❧ (November 1980)

When I initially picked up the novel *The Substitute Guest* by Grace Livingston Hill; I had no idea that my life was about to change forever. I did not know that it was indeed a Christian novel, but God knew.

My life was being transformed while I read the pages of this book. I hadn't finished reading when God stepped into my world and saved me by His grace. My life would never be the same.

That day I realized that there was absolutely no length that God would not go to bring His grace to me, nor to you. I understood personally what Apostle Paul meant when he stated, *O the depths of the riches both of the wisdom and knowledge of God! How unsearchable are his judgments, and his ways past finding out! (Romans 11:33)*

The following week after my conversion, God inspired me to write my testimony in a poetic format. I entitled it *My Substitute*

Guest. Shortly after that, He led me to write *The Pilgrim Tract Society* and ask them to publish the poem. I was a little fearful, to be honest, but I did it anyway. I received a positive response within a brief period.

The poem was initially published and released into circulation as a gospel tract. Then later published in a Southern Christian magazine during the Easter holidays. Since that time(1980) my testimony has been all over the world. I thank God for His grace upon my life. To God be the glory.

It is so important that we are thankful and use all the gifts and talents that God has given us. The ways God desires to use us are without number and the grace to use these gifts are endless. They not only change others lives, but our lives as well. It is my prayer that my testimony of grace be an inspiration to you, to know God and to continue to know Him.

I thank God for the life work and legacy of Ms. Grace Livingston Hill which continues to go on worldwide. My life was changed because of her obedience. Her book, *The Substitute Guest* was copyrighted in 1936.

May God continue to bless and honor the memory of this great Woman of God.

Dedicated To The loving Memory of Ms. Grace Livingston Hill

My Substitute Guest
By
Vanessa Winfield Bonner

For God so loved the world that He gave His only begotten Son, that whosoever believeth in Him should not perish but have everlasting life.
St. John 3:16

I'd heard it said over and over again
But not enough for me to
repent of my sins
I'd say Jesus loves me and
I'd keep on going
Yet He allowed me to live
on - another morning

Deep down I'd known Him once before
He always seemed to knock
on my heart's door
But I closed my mind: I closed my heart
Jesus was calling but I sought Him not

I kept reading as my Bible lay
I said to myself I'll read it one day
Never thought what if that
day never came
For I knew I'd have only me to blame

Then one day as I lay down to rest
I stumbled upon a novel,
"The Substitute Guest"
It was about a family who believed in God
I read this book without a nod

This Christian family their love and trust
I knew for me this was a must

When the stranger in this book asked
How this perfect love was so
They told him of Christ
Who so long ago

Died on the cross for all our sins
That we might open our hearts
And let him come in

This stranger accepted Jesus
And so did I- because He lives
I shall never die
For God knew my heart
But I knew not the rest-
It was he who came
As "My Substitute Guest"

Now I read my Bible everyday
I try to live my life in a Christlike way
I never have to wipe my Bible for dust
Reading God's Word is a daily must

I thank Him for being so loving to me
For opening my eyes- when
I could not see
Christ knew my heart but I
didn't know the rest
It was He who came as "My
Substitute Guest"

❦ (The Invitation) ❦

If you would like to commit your life to Christ, or if you would like to recommit your life to Christ please pray this prayer:

Lord Jesus, I ask you to come into my heart. Forgive me for all my sins. I believe that you are the Son of God and that you died on the cross for my sins. I receive you now as Lord and Savior of my life. I believe that I am saved and that my name is written in the Lamb's book of life. Thank you for saving (restoring) me now.

In Jesus Name, Amen

(Name)

(Date)

❧ About the Author ❧

Vanessa Bonner is an ordained minister and Teacher of God's Word with a heart for Evangelism. She has served in ministry over thirty years and has Pastored in successful house ministries in her community. She is a native of Belhaven, N.C. She received her Bachelor's Degree of Ministry from Covenant Theological Seminary in Greenville, N.C. where she graduated with honors.

She is married to Ronald Bonner. They have three adult children and eight grandchildren. She is Co-founder of Families for Christ outreach ministry in Chocowinity, North Carolina.

She is the author of two previous inspirational books, *"Help God I'm Single but I Don't Want To Be" Copyright 2004 and "One Final Push" Copyright 2009.*

Contact Information

Vanessa W. Bonner
P.O. Box 83
Chocowinity, N.C. 27817

Email: vbonner56@gmail.com

Books by the Author

Help God I'm Single But Don't Want To Be
© 2004

One Final Push © 2009

Notes